ALTERNATOR
BOOKS™

···TECH·TITANS

THE GENIUS OF
FACEBOOK

How Mark Zuckerberg and Social Media Changed the World

Dionna L. Mann

Lerner Publications ◆ Minneapolis

Lerner Publications Company
An imprint of Lerner Publishing Group, Inc.
241 First Avenue North
Minneapolis, MN 55401 USA

For reading levels and more information, look up this title at www.lernerbooks.com.

Main body text set in Aptifer Sans LT Pro.
Typeface provided by Linotype AG.

Library of Congress Cataloging-in-Publication Data

Names: Mann, Dionna L., author.
Title: The genius of Facebook : how Mark Zuckerberg and social media changed the world / Dionna L. Mann.
Description: Minneapolis : Lerner Publications, [2022] | Series: Tech titans (Alternator books) | Includes bibliographical references and index. | Audience: Ages 8–12 | Audience: Grades 4–6 | Summary: "Social media is everywhere. But the boom arguably started when Mark Zuckerberg helped to found Facebook in 2004. Learn more about how Facebook conquered the world and invited controversy along the way in this overview"— Provided by publisher.
Identifiers: LCCN 2021020594 (print) | LCCN 2021020595 (ebook) | ISBN 9781728440804 (library binding) | ISBN 9781728449524 (paperback) | ISBN 9781728445250 (ebook)
Subjects: LCSH: Facebook (Electronic resource)—Juvenile literature. | Zuckerberg, Mark, 1984—-Juvenile literature. | Facebook (Firm)—Juvenile literature. | Online social networks—United States—History—Juvenile literature.
Classification: LCC HM743.F33 M24 2022 (print) | LCC HM743.F33 (ebook) | DDC 302.30285—dc23

LC record available at https://lccn.loc.gov/2021020594
LC ebook record available at https://lccn.loc.gov/2021020595

Manufactured in the United States of America
1 – CG – 7/15/22

TABLE OF CONTENTS

Due to colorblindness, Mark Zuckerberg has trouble distinguishing shades of green and red. Blue is the color he sees best. That's why Facebook's logo is blue!

Twelve-year-old Mark Zuckerberg was hard at work inside his family's home in Dobbs Ferry, New York. He was connecting all the computers in his house, including those inside his dad's attached dentist's office. He was creating a way for his family and his father's staff to instantly message one another—long before instant messaging became popular. They called Mark's home network ZuckNet, and the Zuckerbergs found it very handy.

Little did Mark's family realize that ZuckNet was just the beginning. While still a teenager, Mark would create Facebook, a networking platform that would go on to connect billions of people online.

Dobbs Ferry is near New York City, about 20 miles (32 km) north of Manhattan.

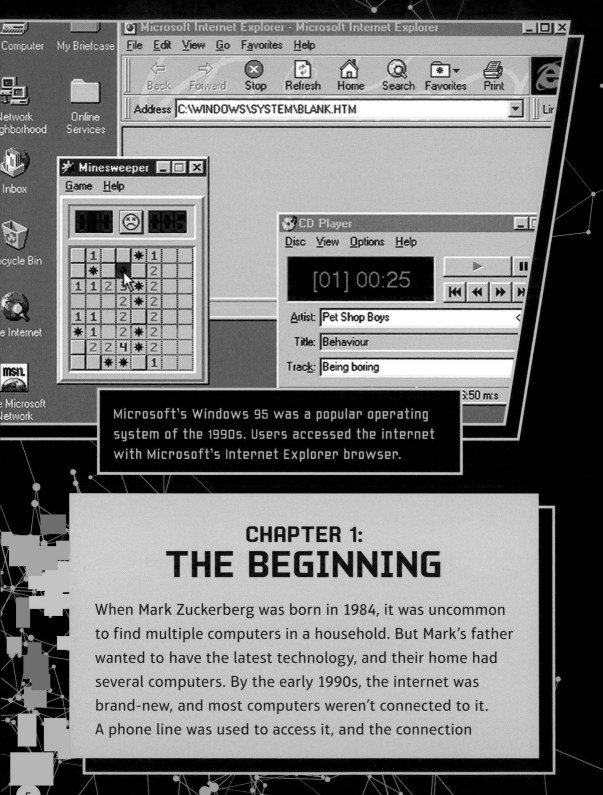

Microsoft's Windows 95 was a popular operating system of the 1990s. Users accessed the internet with Microsoft's Internet Explorer browser.

CHAPTER 1:
THE BEGINNING

When Mark Zuckerberg was born in 1984, it was uncommon to find multiple computers in a household. But Mark's father wanted to have the latest technology, and their home had several computers. By the early 1990s, the internet was brand-new, and most computers weren't connected to it. A phone line was used to access it, and the connection was slow. Even so, the Zuckerbergs' home computers were connected to the World Wide Web.

Young Mark was intrigued by how computers could connect and communicate with one another. When he was about ten years old, Mark began learning the language of computers, or code. He soon figured out that tweaking the code of a piece of technology could make the device do something it wasn't designed to do.

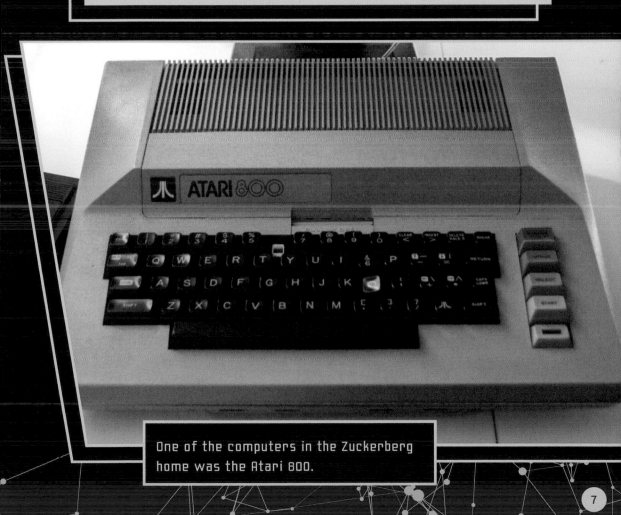

One of the computers in the Zuckerberg home was the Atari 800.

EARLY CODING PROJECTS

Mark started to design his own computer programs for fun. He created a computerized snowball fight to play with his older sister, Randi. He coded a game to conquer Julius Caesar (he never won). He also designed a computer program to prank his mom, who was worried about Y2K, an event some thought would cause all computers to crash as the year 2000 began.

Mark learned coding in many ways. His family's Atari 800 computer had come with an instructional disk about programming. His parents got him a coding tutor when he was eleven. As a young teenager, he attended a college graduate class on coding. Once enrolled at Phillips Exeter Academy, a private high school, he was able to be with other computer geeks. But the main reasons Mark excelled at writing code were that he loved doing it, he spent a lot of time doing it, and his friends were eager to use the programs he created.

Randi Zuckerberg worked for Facebook in the company's early years, acting as a spokesperson and director of marketing.

In his senior year at Exeter, Mark and classmate Adam D'Angelo created an MP3 player with a program that sent song suggestions to a computer. They called it Synapse. Tech companies offered to buy it. But the teens eventually uploaded the source code online, where it was free for anyone to use.

OPEN SOURCE

Many believe the source code of beneficial software should be openly shared. This means that anyone can view, copy, alter, or use the code for free. Over the years, Facebook has been a major contributor of so-called open-source projects. Many companies, such as Netflix, Uber, and Airbnb, have benefited from using Facebook's open-source code.

Netflix is a subscription streaming service that offers thousands of movies and TV shows.

HARVARD

Zuckerberg started college at Harvard University in Cambridge, Massachusetts. There, he worked with other students to create more programs, including Coursematch and Facesmash. Coursematch was a way for other Harvard students to see what courses their peers were taking. Facesmash rated classmates according to their looks, getting Zuckerberg in trouble with Harvard's administration.

In February 2004, during his sophomore year, Zuckerberg coded a program called thefacebook.com. It was an online directory for Harvard students to connect with one another. Students uploaded their profiles, which included their likes and dislikes, their classes, and their relationship status. Students could also "friend" one another. The platform became popular. Soon, students at other colleges wanted an online facebook too.

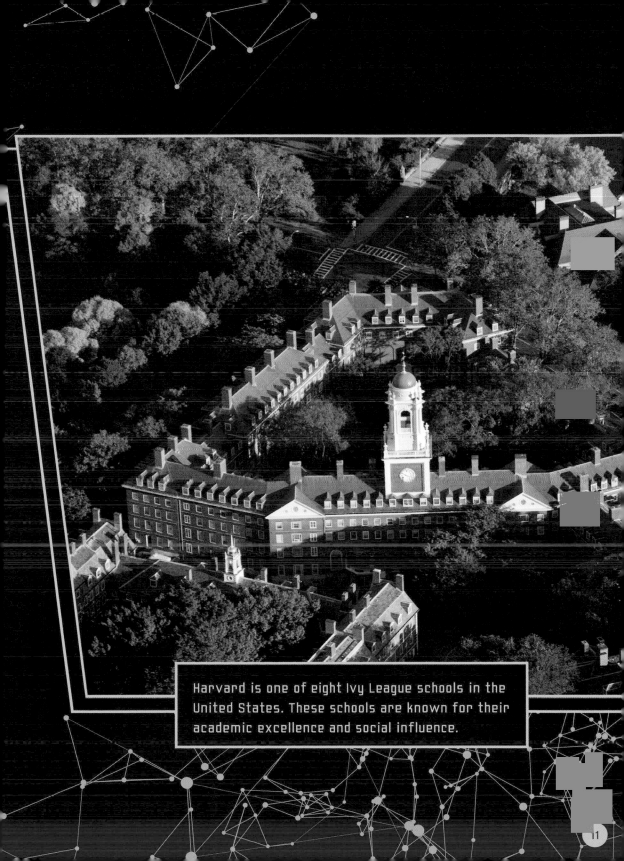

Harvard is one of eight Ivy League schools in the United States. These schools are known for their academic excellence and social influence.

Within months, thefacebook.com was up and running at several universities. Zuckerberg and fellow Harvard students—his roommates, Dustin Moskovitz and Chris Hughes, along with Eduardo Saverin and Andrew McCollum—formed it into a company. Zuckerberg left Harvard and began working on Facebook full-time. The company began receiving millions of dollars in investments.

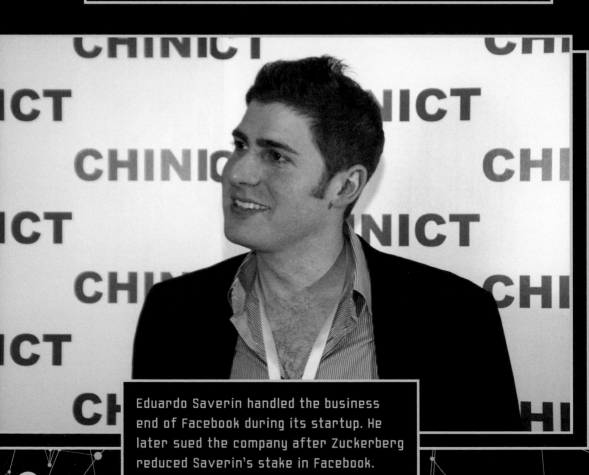

Eduardo Saverin handled the business end of Facebook during its startup. He later sued the company after Zuckerberg reduced Saverin's stake in Facebook.

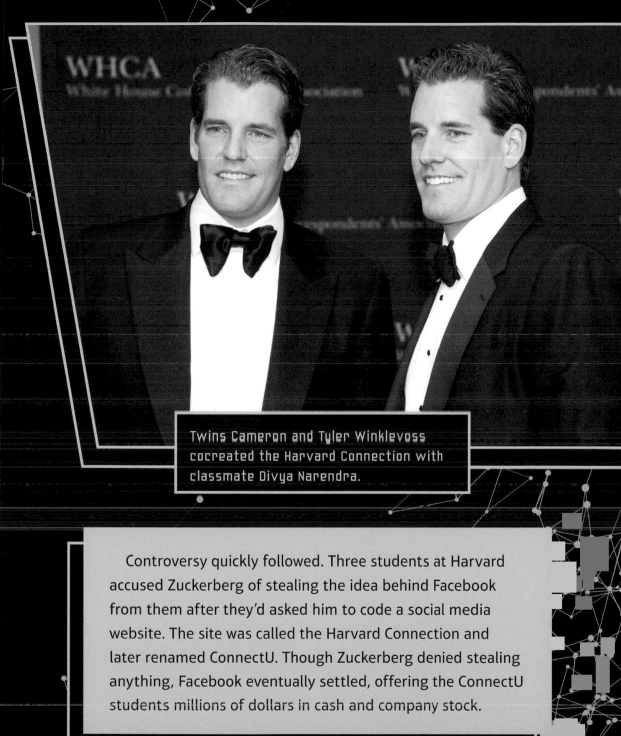

Twins Cameron and Tyler Winklevoss cocreated the Harvard Connection with classmate Divya Narendra.

Controversy quickly followed. Three students at Harvard accused Zuckerberg of stealing the idea behind Facebook from them after they'd asked him to code a social media website. The site was called the Harvard Connection and later renamed ConnectU. Though Zuckerberg denied stealing anything, Facebook eventually settled, offering the ConnectU students millions of dollars in cash and company stock.

Early on, Facebook users could "like" others' posts by clicking a thumbs-up icon. In 2015, Facebook gave users more ways to react to content by introducing various emojis.

CHAPTER 2:
STANDOUT PRODUCTS

Facebook has grown into a powerful company worth billions of dollars. Their social networking platform, with more than two billion active monthly users worldwide, is the main arm of the company. On Facebook, people share personal updates, photos, interests, and opinions with their family, friends, and followers. People use the platform to find and connect with others who have common hobbies, occupations, and viewpoints.

Fans use Facebook to keep tabs on celebrities, sports teams, upcoming movies, and books. Trendsetters use it to endorse products, promote the latest fashions, share their favorite recipes, and more. News junkies use Facebook to stay informed about world events, often tuning into live news feeds. Businesses use Facebook to generate interest in their products, share details about future launches, and create highly targeted advertising.

Social media influencers use Facebook Live to broadcast real-time videos for their followers.

ACQUISITIONS

In 2012, Facebook acquired Instagram, a photo- and video-sharing social media service. In 2014, it acquired WhatsApp, a mobile messaging app that uses Wi-Fi to make phone calls and send videos, pictures, and texts for free. Over time, Facebook has spent more than $23 billion acquiring more than seventy software, tech, and mobile application companies.

In 2020, the Federal Trade Commission (FTC) sued Facebook. The commission claimed that Facebook was engaging in anticompetitive behavior by acquiring Instagram and WhatsApp. Anticompetitive behavior means that Facebook was making it more difficult for small companies to compete with it by buying out its competition and becoming a monopoly.

While Facebook users can engage with the platform in a variety of ways, Instagram is mainly for posting photos and videos.

TWITTER

Twitter is a social media platform similar to Facebook. But while Facebook posts are like message boards that linger, Twitter posts, or tweets, are short and move quickly in and out of the main feed. On Facebook, you "friend" people and "share" and "like" posts. On Twitter, you "follow" people, "retweet," and "heart" posts. On Facebook, posts have no text limit. On Twitter, tweets have a 280-character limit. Both platforms use hashtags to group together posts on the same topic. Facebook has billions of users worldwide. Twitter has millions.

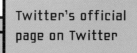

Twitter's official page on Twitter

BEYOND SOCIAL MEDIA

Outside of social media, Facebook also owns subsidiaries that work on hardware for virtual reality (VR) and augmented reality (AR), as well as companies devoted to artificial intelligence (AI). One of these companies is Oculus, which creates and sells VR gaming headsets that make players feel as if they've stepped into an imaginary 3D world.

Oculus showed off its VR headset at San Francisco's Game Developers Conference shortly before Facebook acquired the company in 2014.

C++

One of the back-end computing languages Facebook uses is C++. C++ was developed in the 1980s by Bjarne Stroustrup, a Danish computer scientist. Compared to most other programming languages, C++ allows for faster communication between software and hardware. C++ is standardized, with many libraries of code available for programmers to use. For these reasons, software and hardware developers around the world opt to use C++ for their projects.

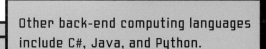

Other back-end computing languages include C#, Java, and Python.

Zuckerberg speaking at a 2018 press conference in Paris, France

CHAPTER 3:
IN THE NEWS

From the time of Facebook's founding in 2004, Zuckerberg and his company have made headlines. Early on, people were eager to learn more about the young entrepreneur who had quickly made millions. In 2008, Zuckerberg was recognized as the youngest self-made billionaire at the age of twenty-three. In 2010, he was named Person of the Year by *Time* magazine and appeared on the cover.

PHILANTHROPY

Since making his fortune, Zuckerberg and his wife, Priscilla Chan, have been in the news for their philanthropy. In 2010, Zuckerberg donated $100 million to help the public school system in Newark, New Jersey. He appeared on *The Oprah Winfrey Show* to talk about it. In 2020, he and Chan made the news again when they donated $300 million to protect US elections.

Priscilla Chan (*above*) and Zuckerberg started the Chan Zuckerberg Initiative with the goal of solving some of society's biggest problems and building a healthy, just future for everyone.

MISINFORMATION & PRIVACY VIOLATION

Facebook has had its share of bad press too. Many institutions have blamed the platform for allowing users to negatively influence free elections, ignite ethnic tensions, and fuel civil and political unrest. While having a Facebook account does give a user the freedom to use their voice, Facebook has a set of community standards that users agree to follow. This allows the company to police its content and remove posts that encourage violence, spout hate speech, or spread false or misleading information that endangers the public.

In 2018, with live cameras rolling, Zuckerberg faced a US Senate Committee for the first time. Facebook had experienced a huge breach in user privacy. An app developer got permission to collect Facebook user data, but then, without consent, sold the data to another party, Cambridge Analytica. Cambridge Analytica then

Misinformation that spread through Facebook and other online communities led many Americans to believe without proof that the 2020 election results were fraudulent.

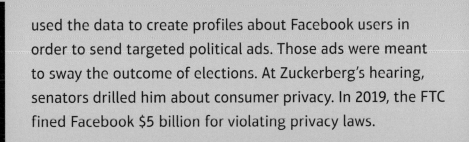

used the data to create profiles about Facebook users in order to send targeted political ads. Those ads were meant to sway the outcome of elections. At Zuckerberg's hearing, senators drilled him about consumer privacy. In 2019, the FTC fined Facebook $5 billion for violating privacy laws.

Mr. Mark Zuckerberg

Zuckerberg testifying before the US Senate in April 2018

Facebook set up a VR display pop-up in Chicago's Millennium Park in 2016.

CHAPTER 4:
A LOOK AHEAD

Facebook Reality Labs is invested in futuristic technology. Its engineers are developing human–computer interaction platforms. A large amount of its research involves wearable tech with AR. They're working on innovative VR experiences that engage the senses, and useful AI applications too.

TIKTOK

TikTok is a social media platform where users share short videos. TikTok's app includes templates, music, filters, and editing features for video creation. On Facebook, hashtags are about finding conversations occurring around a certain topic. On TikTok, hashtags help users connect in real-time, whether that's by telling jokes, offering tips, or accepting video challenges. Some of the most popular challenges on TikTok invite users to quickly upload videos of themselves doing certain dance moves.

In September 2021, TikTok reported having one billion users worldwide.

AR & VR

Facebook Reality Labs engineers are developing lightweight AR glasses designed to overlay computer-generated images and suggestions onto the wearer's real-world vision. The glasses will include smart audio to cancel out unwanted background noise while amplifying desired sounds.

Facebook Reality Labs is also developing specialized headsets that will take virtual sounds to a new level. Spatialized audio and simulated acoustics within the VR headset will make computer-generated sounds seem as though they are occurring in real time and space. With visual and audio components, the headsets could make it seem as though far-away people are gathered in the same room.

Facebook Reality Labs is working on VR-headset simulations for educational purposes too. One example is first responder training. In the VR training, a responder learns how to make quick, smart decisions in a lifelike emergency situation. These simulations can help medical students become effective caregivers in the real world.

Zuckerberg's vision of Facebook becoming a tool for the human family to connect via the internet to say hello, exchange ideas, and share their news has certainly become a reality—a ZuckNet stretching around the world.

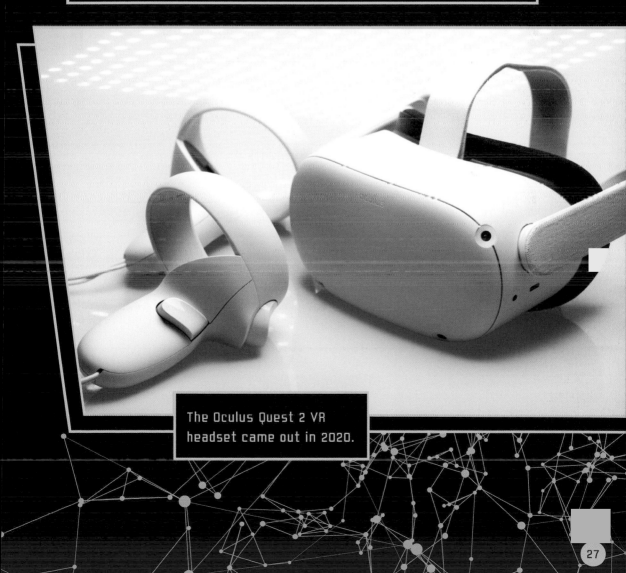

The Oculus Quest 2 VR headset came out in 2020.

TIMELINE

2004: Mark Zuckerberg launches thefacebook.com at Harvard University.

2006: Facebook opens to anyone thirteen years or older with a valid email.

2008: Facebook reaches a settlement with the creators of the Harvard Connection, later named ConnectU.

2010: A movie about Facebook's rise, called *The Social Network*, is released.

February 2012: Facebook becomes a publicly traded and owned entity.

April 2012:	Facebook acquires Instagram for $1 billion.
2014:	Facebook acquires WhatsApp for $19 billion (in cash and stocks).
2018:	Zuckerberg testifies before members of the US Senate regarding data privacy and protection.
2019:	Facebook gets a $5 billion penalty from the Federal Trade Commission for violating privacy laws.
2021:	Facebook announces that it is changing its name to Meta.

GLOSSARY

acquire: to purchase 51 percent or more of a smaller company's shares, taking control of the smaller company

artificial intelligence (AI): a computer system that imitates human thought to process information

augmented reality (AR): an experience that combines real-world sights, sounds, and activities with computer-generated information

breach: a break, infraction, or violation of law or obligation toward another party

entrepreneur: a person who starts a business and is willing to risk loss to make money

hashtag: a word or phrase preceded by the symbol # that categorizes the accompanying text

monopoly: a company that has complete ownership or control of the supply of goods or services in a certain market

philanthropy: an act done or gift made for humanitarian purposes

simulate: to create a situation or event that seems real but is fabricated to help people deal with such situations or events if they were to occur in the future

subsidiary: a company controlled or owned by another company

virtual reality (VR): an artificial environment with sounds and sights created by a computer

LEARN MORE

Anton, Carrie. *A Smart Girl's Guide: Digital World: How to Connect, Share, Play, and Keep Yourself Safe.* Middleton, WI: American Girl Publishing, 2017.

Facebook
https://kids.britannica.com/students/article/Facebook/544333

Gregory, Josh. *Posting on Social Media.* New York: Children's Press, 2019.

Kawa, Katie. *Mark Zuckerberg: Founder of Facebook.* New York: PowerKids Press, 2017.

Mark Zuckerberg
https://kids.britannica.com/students/article/Mark
-Zuckerberg/607336

Mattern, Joanne. *Facebook.* Minneapolis: Abdo Publishing, 2017.

Scratch Tutorials
https://scratch.mit.edu/projects/editor/?tutorial=getStarted

Teaching Kids to Be Smart About Social Media
https://kidshealth.org/en/parents/social-media-smarts.html

INDEX

PHOTO ACKNOWLEDGMENTS

The images in this book are used with the permission of: © Frederic Legrand/Shutterstock Images, p. 4; © Jim.henderson/Wikimedia Commons, p. 5; © John Pasden/Flickr, p. 6; © Gary L Hider/Shutterstock Images, p. 7; © ANDREW KELLY/Wikimedia Commons, p. 8; © sitthiphong/Shutterstock Images, p. 9; © Joseph Sohm/Shutterstock Images, p. 11; © Gravesv38/Wikimedia Commons, p. 12; © Rena Schild/Shutterstock Images, p. 13; © Jakraphong Photography/Shutterstock Images, p. 14; © Artem Varnitsin/Shutterstock Images, p. 15; © Jirapong Manustrong/Shutterstock Images, pp. 16, 17; © Barone Firenze/Shutterstock Images, p. 18; © Monstar Studio/Shutterstock Images, p. 19; © Frederic Legrand - COMEO/Shutterstock Images, p. 20; © Steve Jennings/Wikimedia Commons, p. 21; © Johnny Silvercloud/Shutterstock Images, p. 22; © The Photo Access/Alamy Photo, p. 23; © Big Joe/Shutterstock Images, p. 24; © Nattakorn_Maneerat/Shutterstock Images, p. 25; © Boumen Japet/Shutterstock Images, p. 27.

Cover Photos: © Barone Firenze/Shutterstock Images (Facebook sign); © Kaspars Grinvalds/Shutterstock Images (login page); © Star Max 2/AP Images (Mark Zuckerberg)

Design Elements: © Hluboki Dzianis/Shutterstock Images